Jesus for Sceptics

Michael Green

Illustrations by Ruth Cunningham

a bethinking book

Madness to believe?
Folly to reject?

I have written this book because I am tired of meeting people who dismiss Jesus Christ with a wave of the hand but have never looked into the evidence for themselves. There are many weighty tomes on the subject. I wanted to offer you something brief but accurate and arresting. You must decide whether or not I have succeeded. There are endless discussions about various aspects of Christianity and unbelief. In this short book I leave them on one side and go to the heart of the matter, Jesus Christ himself. I respect sceptics who are open to evidence, and so I concentrate on such questions as, 'Who was Jesus?' 'Have we any reliable information about him?' 'Why was he killed?' 'Is the resurrection possible?' 'What difference could he make to my life?'

If those are some of your questions, read on!

Michael Green
Oxford, 2013

one
scepticism

scepticism

We live in a sceptical age.

We are sceptical about politics, so millions do not vote. Sceptical about the police, apparently ridden with corruption and racism. Sceptical about the media, what with phone tapping and the twisting of news. Sceptical about almost all the traditional virtues – except tolerance.

We are certainly sceptical about Christianity. To be sure, it has been the background of our culture, but now it looks threadbare. If we are to believe the New Atheists, there is no God. If we are to believe our eyes, churches are largely empty. The record of the church as an institution is, at best, patchy. There have been many great things in its history like the promotion of education, the building of hospitals and the liberation of slaves. But there have also been terrible scandals like obscurantism, the Crusades, the Galileo affair, corruption in its leadership, neglect of the poor, and recently the widespread sexual abuse of children. So it is not surprising that there is today a climate of scepticism about the Christian church. I understand that and, to a large extent, I share it. We Christians must put our hands up and acknowledge our part in the massive failures of the church.

That said, the heart of Christianity is Jesus Christ. The behaviour of Christians does not affect its truth claims, but remove Jesus from Christianity and the whole religion, the largest the world has ever seen, would collapse like a pack of cards. The only thing that distinguished Christianity from Judaism in the early days was the person of Jesus Christ. The only thing that distinguishes Christianity today from the morality and social concern of generous atheists is the person of Jesus Christ. And so here is our question: have the acids of cynicism and scepticism eaten him away?

Often, when I am commending the cause of Jesus Christ in some university or public meeting, I meet people who say something to this effect: 'Well, if you can believe that stuff, good for you. I am very sceptical about the whole thing.' My reply rarely fails to surprise, as I say, 'I am delighted to hear you are sceptical. That's a great place to start enquiries.'

I am not being facetious, but utterly sincere. The word 'scepticism' has a long and distinguished history. There's nothing intrinsically wrong with scepticism. The word takes us back to the ancient Greeks, and simply means 'investigation' or 'consideration' (*skepsis*). The sceptic refuses to take a dogmatic position but prefers to keep an open mind. And there is nothing disreputable about an open mind – so long as it is not open at both ends! It was G.K. Chesterton who once quipped, 'The object of opening the mind, as of opening the mouth, is to shut it again on something solid.' An excellent example of the proper use of scepticism is provided by Xenophanes, the earliest of the pre-Socratic philosophers in the sixth century BC. He doubted, reasonably enough, whether you could know anything outside the realm of personal experience: but you could have opinions. He attacked the traditional polytheism, with its many gods and their lusts and battles, which led him to believe that people created gods in their own image, concluding that if horses could draw they would draw their gods looking like horses! Instead, he proposed belief in one god, and deduced the properties of such a god from what was 'fitting'.

But while scepticism properly means the open-minded

examination of a topic, and refusal to be swayed by tradition or sentiment, in today's culture it has come to have a negative meaning. It can be applied to a theory, or to any proposed course of action like military intervention, or to supposed beings like ghosts and fairies. But most commonly it is applied to religion. Christianity is the one most commonly singled out for attack. A sceptic is someone who does not believe it. He or she might possibly be persuaded if the evidence is shown to be

good enough, but usually, no, the sceptic remains an unbeliever.

In many ways scepticism is healthy. It means you refuse to be taken for a ride. You refuse to credit anything where the evidence is weak. You are not easily conned. You want to be persuaded that the intellectual ice will bear your weight before stepping out on it. Excellent.

Scepticism cannot, however, be a default position and if it becomes so will cease to be healthy at all. After all you can't doubt a thing until there is something to doubt. Scepticism is always secondary to belief: you have to believe something before you can doubt it. Doubt about God, for example, depends on the prior existence of belief in God. Scepticism simply cannot stand on its own, so if my attitude to life is dominated by scepticism it will make me a negative, perhaps rather sour individual. The famous Scottish philosopher David Hume lived in the eighteenth century, but his influence remains powerful today. Hume was a profound sceptic, being highly dubious about the link between cause and effect, and even about personal identity! He reckoned there was no such thing as the self: we are nothing but 'a collection of different perspectives which succeed one another with inconceivable rapidity, and are in perpetual flux and movement'. If that is your worldview, if like Hume you are 'ready to reject all belief and reasoning, and can look on no opinion even as more probable or likely than another', then it is hardly surprising that you can easily become negative and sour! In Hume's case, he was rescued by his humanity. He tells us, 'Most fortunately it happens that since reason is incapable of dispelling these clouds, nature herself suffices to that purpose. A few hours of good company and backgammon,' he tells us, 'made my melancholy and sceptical conclusions seem ridiculous!'

You may doubt the existence of God, though the evidence for him is strong. You may doubt the vitality of the church, though worldwide it is growing at over 70,000 a day. You may doubt the usefulness of Christianity, which seems to you to make little difference to the lives of many who profess it. But you can hardly doubt everything at once! So I want to leave the other objections to Christianity aside for the moment, and concentrate attention in this short book on the very heart of the Christian faith, Jesus Christ himself. And I want to encourage you, if you are something of a sceptic, to adopt that open mind which the word really alludes to. Examine the evidence for yourself, and consider whether Jesus might, rather than being a source for doubt, actually be a solid base on which to build a confident life in a confusing world.

two
sceptical about whether
Jesus ever lived?

sceptical
about whether
Jesus ever live

If I were to claim that Julius Caesar or Alexander the Great never lived, you would think me crazy. Such an idea never crosses anyone's mind. Jesus of Nazareth is far more famous and has had a far greater influence than either Alexander or Caesar, and yet you will find people who deny he ever existed! I wonder if that is a form of escapism?

For years G.A.Wells, a professor of German in Birkbeck College London, insisted that Jesus never existed. Then there was John Allegro who argued, apparently seriously, that the whole Christian movement arose from the use of hallucinogenic mushrooms. Such bizarre suggestions do not last for long, but there has been a sceptical strain going back to Sir James George Frazer's *Golden Bough*, that Christianity was nothing more than one of the old mystery religions, which are largely forgotten nowadays but were very influential in the Roman Empire. The main difference between them and Christianity, so the theory goes, was that Christianity succeeded! And so you find Tom Harpur in *The Pagan Christ* asserting, 'There is nothing the Jesus of the Gospels said and did … that cannot be shown to have originated thousands of years before in the Egyptian mystery rites and other sacred liturgies.' 'Nothing in Christianity is original,' claims Dan Brown in *The Da Vinci Code*. The book maintains that, although Jesus was a historical figure, everything of importance in Christianity was taken directly from earlier pagan mystery religions. I even recall debating with a man in the University of Florida in 2007 who held the same position.

If this argument is to be more than a lazy polemic we must look at what these mystery religions were. They were a varied bunch of religious movements from the Eastern Mediterranean that flourished in the early Roman Empire, and grew out of age-old fertility cults and nature worship. People were fascinated by the successive rise, flowering, decay and rebirth of the seasons of the year, and applied them to human life. After a century of civil war preceding the start of the Empire, belief in the traditional gods of Rome had decayed, and there was a widespread hunger for security, significance and meaning. Many people turned to the mystery religions in their search for spiritual support, close companionship and the hope of life after death. They were called 'mystery religions' because they were closed societies whose initiates were sworn to secrecy, which is why we do not know a great deal about them. We do know that they had sacred rites, a common meal and a special meeting place. They had, like Christianity, a hunger for salvation, but that salvation was rescue from the cold hand of Fate and (usually) from the terrors of the after-life, not from sin and self-centredness.

In the past, some scholars drew attention to a number of similarities between these mystery religions and Christian beliefs and lifestyle, and suggested that Christianity emerged from these cults. In recent years, however, a lot of careful research has been done on these various mystery religions by scholars Ronald Nash, T.N.D. Mettinger and others, which has shown conclusively that none of these mystery religions provide convincing parallels to Jesus. Indeed, I doubt whether you could find any competent scholar nowadays who maintains that Christianity was either derived from or influenced by the mystery religions. The essential difference between them and Christianity was simple. It lay in the person of Jesus of Nazareth.

Demeter, Adonis, Osiris, Mithras, Dionysus and the rest were all mythical figures – nobody believed they had actually lived. They were invented to explain some aspect of life, sexuality or death. In striking contrast, however, Jesus was a recent and well-attested historical figure, whom the first preachers of the Christian message had known personally. This is absolutely crucial and sets Jesus apart from all the mythological saviour figures of the mystery cults. Not only were none of their heroes historical, but there is absolutely no suggestion in any of the mystery religions that the god dies and is resurrected in order to lead the faithful to eternal life. Many of the alleged parallels which intrigued earlier scholars have now been shown to be post-Christian and therefore cannot possibly have affected the rise of Christianity. There remains the very obvious fact that Christianity emerged in a distinctive and passionately monotheistic Jewish environment that would not touch any pagan religions with a barge pole. The idea that Christianity began as one of the mystery religions has been totally discredited.

It is worth pausing a moment on the historical nature of the Christian faith. Religions such as Buddhism or Confucianism would continue to flourish even if it could be proved that Buddha or Confucius never lived. It is their teaching that matters. But that is not the case with Christianity, which is not a system of religious rituals and ethics. It is essentially good news about a unique historical person, who died a mere thirty years or so before the Gospels began to appear. Lots of eyewitnesses were still around who could have checked their accounts. If you could show that Jesus never lived, Christianity would collapse like a pricked balloon. For it all depends on the conviction that this person, Jesus of Nazareth, who claimed to share God's nature as well as our own, was a historical figure about whom we can know a good deal.

This claim is a matter not of ideology or mythology, but of history. What, then, is the historical evidence for Jesus? It comes both from Christian and non-Christian sources.

Christian evidence

The earliest evidence comes from the followers of Jesus themselves, and is contained in the four Gospels and the letters of the apostles Paul, Peter, James and John. Written in the second half of the first century as the eyewitness generation was beginning to age, the Gospels bring us the oral proclamation of previous decades, and they represent an entirely new form of literature. They are not, strictly speaking, biographies or histories, though they contain both biography and history. They are, as the name 'gospel' indicates, 'good news' documents, good news about this Jesus who had revolutionised the lives of their authors and a great many others. Needless to say, with so much at stake, the veracity of the Gospels has been under constant attack, yet today their stock remains as high as ever. I do not ask you to regard them as inspired scripture, beyond criticism or error, but simply to evaluate them as the honest attempts of contemporaries to bear testimony to the life, death and resurrection of the most amazing person the world had ever seen, the man who split history in two. There is, after all, no other great man who can boast of a third of the human race worshipping him two thousand years after his death!

You may feel that their evidence must be prejudiced. You cannot believe the Gospels? Very well, look for some corroborating evidence about the historicity of Jesus in secular sources. Four non-Christian authors, writing within seventy years of his death, tell us something about him.

Roman evidence

The earliest is Thallus, who was a Samaritan and possibly a freedman of the Emperor Tiberius. Living in Rome, he set out by AD 52 to write a history of the world from the Trojan War until his own day. Amazingly he included a reference to the darkness which the Gospels tell us engulfed the land at the death of Jesus (Mark 15.33). Though the rest of Thallus' work is lost, this fragment survives. It shows that the story of Jesus' death was known in secular circles in Rome in the middle of the first century. Indeed in AD 49 the Emperor Claudius, exasperated by the constant riots among the large Jewish community in Rome, banished Jews from the city. Among writers who mention this is Luke who tells us in Acts 18.2 that when Paul arrived in Corinth (about AD 50) he found 'a Jew named Aquila, a native of Pontus, lately come from Italy with his wife Priscilla, because Claudius had commanded all the Jews to leave Rome.' Suetonius, a highly placed secretary under the Emperor Hadrian, adds that this was because the Jews were 'constantly rioting at the instigation of one Chrestus' (*Life of Claudius* 25). Chrestus was a common mis-spelling for the name of Christ. It seems that Suetonius slightly misunderstood the situation, which had taken place twenty years before he was born. He thought that Chrestus was orchestrating the riots, whereas in fact the riots reflect tensions in the large Jewish community in Rome as debates about Christ made their impact. So if Claudius' patience gave out in AD 49 and he issued the expulsion order, there must have been substantial numbers of Christians in Rome in the forties of the first century, that is to say only a decade after the death of Jesus.

The next witness is Mara bar-Serapion who sent a letter from prison to his son in AD 73. The letter, written in Syriac, is preserved in the British Museum. He asks rhetorically what advantage the Athenians gained from putting Socrates to death, or the men of Samos from burning Pythagoras. 'What advantage,' he asks, 'did the Jews gain from executing their wise king?' He points out that their kingdom was abolished shortly afterwards, and that Jesus lived on in the teaching which he had given.

Much the most important Roman witness was Tacitus, the greatest of Roman historians. He wrote towards the end of the first century, some 60 years after the death of Jesus – in *Annals* 15.44 he tells us that Nero unjustly tried to fasten the blame for the Fire of Rome in AD 64 on

the Christians, and burnt them alive. He continued, 'Christus, from whom the name had its origin, suffered the extreme penalty (i.e. execution) during the reign of Tiberius at the hands of one of our procurators, Pontius Pilatus.' You could hardly be more explicit than that! Suetonius also mentions the atrocities against Christians after the great fire (*Life of Nero* 16).

The other significant witness was Pliny the Younger, a Roman aristocrat and man of letters who in AD 112 became governor of the province of Bithynia in north-west Turkey. When he arrived in his province, he came across lots of Christians, and wrote to the Emperor Trajan asking advice on what to do about them. The whole extensive letter (*Epistles* 10.96) is fascinating, particularly the sentence, 'They were in the habit of meeting on a certain fixed day (i.e. Sunday) before it was light, and they sang hymns to Christ as God, and bound themselves by a solemn oath (*sacramentum*) not to commit any wicked deed but to abstain from all fraud, theft and adultery.' Pliny leaves us in no doubt that Jesus was a recent historical figure whom large numbers of people in his province worshipped.

Jewish evidence

Perhaps the most surprising testimony to the historical Jesus comes from the pen of Flavius Josephus. He was a Jewish commander in the war against Rome, and after the defeat of the Jews in AD 70 he set out to re-establish the reputation of Judaism in the minds of Roman society in general and the imperial family (his patrons!) in particular. He did this between AD 75 and 95 by writing two important and lengthy books, *The Antiquities of the Jews* and *The Jewish War*. The following remarkable passage occurs in *Antiquities* 18.3.3.

'There arose about this time [Pilate's time] Jesus, a wise man, if we should call him a man, for he was the doer of marvellous deeds, a teacher of men who receive the truth with pleasure. He led away many Jews, and also many Greeks. This man was the Messiah. And when Pilate had condemned him to the cross, on his impeachment by the chief men among us, those who had loved him at the first did not cease; for he appeared to them on the third day alive again, the divine prophets having spoken these and thousands of wonderful things about him. And even now the tribe of Christians, so named after him, has not yet died out.'

Josephus was certainly not a Christian, so this is an astonishing testimony to find in his writings. Many have assailed its genuineness. But its attestation is as good as anything in Josephus. It is included in all the manuscripts. The early Christian fathers knew it – Eusebius in the fourth century quotes it twice. Probably some of it is sarcastic: 'if we should call him a man' may refer to his divine claims, and 'this man was the Messiah' to the charge affixed to his cross, while the passage about the resurrection may merely be reflecting Christian propaganda. It is possible that the passage has suffered some Christian interpolation. It is more probable, though, that Josephus is producing 'this man was the Messiah' as a sardonic demonstration of the folly of messianic risings, which were plentiful in the first century and which he regarded as the utmost folly. In any case, we have in Josephus a powerful independent testimony to the historical reality of Jesus of Nazareth. The stories about Jesus were no myth. They were so circumstantial and so well documented that they found a place in the work of this Jewish apologist who had the strongest reasons not to annoy his patrons by including anything so inconvenient to his theme!

It is not surprising then, in the light of all this evidence, that as Professor Otto Betz put it, 'No serious scholar has ventured to postulate the non-historicity of Jesus.' Even James Frazer, whose *Golden Bough* sought the origins of Christianity in the mystery religions, concluded that 'the doubts which have been cast on the historical reality of Jesus are, in my judgment, unworthy of attention.'

three

sceptical about the reliability
of the Gospels?

sceptical about the reliability of the Gospels?

I do a good deal of speaking in universities, and whenever the challenge of Jesus to personal commitment looms on the horizon someone is almost bound to exclaim, ' I don't believe the Gospels,' 'They were written centuries later,' or, 'The text is so corrupt that we can't know what the original was like.'

It is astonishing how widespread this idea is. For some, it is undoubtedly an excuse for not wanting to face up to what the Gospels have to say. For others, it is a genuine doubt about their reliability. On any showing, the subject is an important one. If we are to gain any solid knowledge about Jesus we are going to have to use these Gospels, since they are the earliest documents we have. Can we trust them? That is the issue. Let's ask a few questions.

When were the Gospels written?

Nobody who has seriously examined the evidence can doubt that the four Gospels were written in the first century AD. They are quoted extensively in the writings of Clement in the 90s and Ignatius a decade later. Thereafter they are cited one way or another in every Christian document that has come down to us. Most scholars regard Mark's Gospel as the earliest, written in the 60s, followed by Matthew and Luke a decade or so later, with John either in the 80s or possibly, according to a minority of scholars, before AD 70. Precise dating remains a hot topic of scholarly debate, but it is simply not possible to date the Gospels later than the last quarter of the first century. There are very few ancient documents where the records were written so close to the events themselves. If we ask why they were not written earlier still, the answer is twofold. First, the ancients preferred spoken to written testimony; and second, the first Christians were so busy preaching the material contained in the Gospels that they did not think to write it down. It was only as the first generation were getting older that they realised how important it was to record for future generations the material which had so transformed their own lives. At all events, any idea that the Gospels were written in the second century or later is totally impossible. By then they had been so quoted by writers from the end of the first century onwards, and had become so central to the life and faith of the church, that Irenaeus (mid second century) could rate their position as unassailable, like the four winds or the four points of the compass! There was never any doubt about the authenticity of these four Gospels. Their standing and uniqueness is rock solid.

But are there not other Gospels, which were excluded from the Bible?

There are indeed many texts that have not made their way into the Bible, and for good reason. You may be one of the millions who read Dan Brown's entertaining novel, *The Da Vinci Code*, where he makes great play with *The Gospel of Mary* and *The Gospel of Philip*, among others. What is too often forgotten is that his book is just a novel: its theme is fantasy not truth. The books he refers to were recovered from the sands of Egypt in 1945 and were written between the second and fourth century AD by a sect opposed to mainline Christianity. They are not really 'Gospels' at all, since they show no interest in the life and death of Jesus, add nothing to our knowledge of him, and are full of theological psycho-babble promoting a heresy called Gnosticism. They do not come from the eyewitness generation, but were written centuries later and are historically worthless for assessing anything other than third-century Gnostics. None of them was ever part of the Bible, and none of them is relevant to our enquiries about Jesus.

Do we have the text of the four Gospels substantially as it was written?

Very well, let's get back to the four Gospels in our New Testament. Can we believe that our Greek text of the Gospels is what the authors actually wrote? There are, of course, many variant readings as was inevitable in ancient book production, where someone stood out at the front reading a passage whilst a bevy of scribes took down what they heard. There are a great many tiny variations in the Gospel texts, as one might expect from such a procedure, but not one of them overthrows a single Christian doctrine. The clerical errors and differences affect the grammar more than the substance. Even Bart Ehrman, whose controversial book *Misquoting Jesus* emphasises the variety of textual readings, cannot show that any Christian doctrine is jeopardised, and, indeed, there are very few places in the Gospels where there is any serious doubt about the original reading.

One of them is the ending of Mark's Gospel. The earliest

copies we have break off at 16.8 with the awe and amazement of the women surveying the empty tomb. 'They said nothing to anyone, for they were afraid.' Verses 9-20 offer us two additional and alternative endings to the Gospel, provided by early copyists who thought, understandably, that to end with verse 8 was very abrupt. (Mark may have been arrested at that point, perhaps even died, or the last page of his book may have got torn off.) Verses 9-20 are written in an entirely different style, draw together resurrection stories from elsewhere and are clearly an attempt to round off the Gospel. They are missing in our earliest manuscripts, and seem to date from the early second century. But they do not negatively affect the Christian faith in any way, since Mark has already told us that Jesus rose from the dead. We are free, therefore, to reject these verses as historical, but the resurrection itself remains solidly affirmed.

The other place where there is serious doubt concerns the story of Jesus' gracious but firm response to the woman taken in adultery. In most manuscripts it follows John 7.52, but in some is placed after verse 36, or at the end of the Gospel, or even after Luke 21.38. It seems that this story, eminently characteristic of Jesus, was circulating in the early church, and was much valued, but had no secure place in the text of the Gospel, and so various scribes placed it where they thought fit.

Granted that these are the only two places in the Gospels where there is serious doubt about the manuscript tradition, could not the church in later years have monkeyed with the text? We all know the game of 'Chinese whispers' where one person whispers a statement to another, and after it has reached ten or more it turns out to be very different from the original. Could not something similar have happened with the New Testament stories?

The answer is an emphatic no, for this reason. We have more than 5,700 manuscripts of the Greek New Testament, another 10,000 or so in Latin, and a large number in Syriac and Coptic. If there had been additions, subtractions or corruptions they would certainly have shown up by comparing one manuscript with others. But this is not the case. The textual tradition is remarkably constant throughout. We can be confident that we have the material in the Gospels in substantially the same form as the authors wrote it, apart from the minor textual variations mentioned above.

Actually, there are other checks on the text. We have an enormous number of quotations in the ancient church fathers – so many that it would be almost possible to reconstruct the whole New Testament from their writings alone. In addition we have a large number of ancient lectionaries offering additional confirmation. We can be very sure of the text of the New Testament.

How old are our earliest manuscripts?

It is one thing to claim that the textual tradition is almost uniform, which it is, but it is quite another matter to ask how old our earliest extant manuscripts are, and how long they were written after the autograph copies which have, of course, long turned to dust.

The answer is very interesting. Normally the gap between

the original writings and the oldest surviving manuscript is massive. In the case of the great Greek historian Thucydides, for instance, the gap is 1400 years. In the case of Tacitus, the brilliant Roman historian, the gap is 800 years, with Plato 1200 years, and with Julius Caesar 1000 years. But in the case of the Gospels we have a gap of a mere 30 years or so between the publication of John's Gospel and the earliest manuscript evidence we have of it. The fragment is dated between AD 100 and AD 125, and you can go and see it in the John Rylands Library in Manchester. We have Greek manuscripts of the whole of the New Testament written before AD 200. There is no body of ancient literature in the world which enjoys such a wealth of good textual attestation as the New Testament, and none where the gap between the autograph copies and the earliest surviving manuscripts is so small.

Sir Frederic Kenyon, former Director of the British Museum and its Principal Librarian, fittingly concluded, 'The interval between the dates of the original composition and the earliest extant evidence becomes so small as to be in fact negligible, and the last foundation for any doubt that the scriptures have come down to us substantially as they were written has been removed. Both the authenticity and the general integrity of the books of the New Testament may be regarded as finally established.' Granted, Kenyon wrote this in 1901, but nothing in the intervening century has disturbed the truth of his claim.

What about Muslim complaints that the text is corrupt?

If you have had any extensive conversations about faith with Muslims they will have told you that while the Qur'an came directly from heaven to an illiterate Muhammad, the New Testament is full of textual errors and therefore corrupt. Several things need to be said.

In the first place the Qur'an speaks of three tracts of scripture that were revealed before Muhammad – the Law of Moses (e.g. Qur'an sura 3.93), the Psalms (e.g. 4.163) and the Gospels (e.g. 5.46), and Muslims are told to believe these scriptures as well as the Qur'an (sura 3.93; 4.136). But on the other hand there are four verses in the Qur'an which accuse the Jews of 'falsifying' or 'twisting the meaning' of their scriptures (2.75; 4.46; 5.13; 5.41). However, none of them say the text is corrupt, merely that the Jews have twisted it. Nowhere in the Qur'an does it say the Christian scriptures are corrupt – merely on two occasions that Christians have concealed some of what has been revealed to them and have forgotten part of the revelation (2.140; 5.14). Neither of these references account for the deep Muslim conviction that the biblical text is corrupt. In fact that accusation first appeared not in the Qur'an at all but in the eleventh century, particularly in the Muslim apologist, Al-Juwayni! How seriously can you take that?

Second, Muslims and Christians have very different ideas of scripture. For Muslims the Qur'an was revealed perfect and in Arabic to Muhammad, with no possibility of error. Christians hold that scripture is indeed God's revelation, but given to us through a variety of human authors down several centuries. Muslims think God's revelation was given in a perfect book. Christians believe it was given in a perfect person, to whom the Gospel accounts bear witness. This is an enormously significant difference.

Finally it appears that, after all the protestations, the Qur'an does not have a uniform text without variations. The respected (and very courageous) historian Tom Holland has shown in his recent book *In the Shadow of the Sword*, drawing on specialist research, not only that we have no sources at all about Muhammad until two hundred years after his death, but also that today's 'authentic' version of the Qur'an was only established in Cairo in 1924. Before that there were seven equally valid 'readings'. The earliest verses we know of are not in manuscript at all but on the walls of the Dome of the Rock mosque in Jerusalem, built in AD 691 – and they differ from the same verses in today's Qur'an. So the

Islamic holy book has gone through the same process as the Gospels, whose text they regard as corrupt!

We can safely dismiss both the ignorant claims that the Gospels are late and unreliable, and the Muslim claims that the text is corrupt. If we are going to remain sceptical about Jesus, we must do so on other grounds than the Gospel text!

four
sceptical about
who Jesus was?

sceptical about
who Jesus was

The central conviction of a Christian is that Jesus was not only human but shared the nature of God. That seems utterly ridiculous to the sceptic, but, though it may be shocking, perhaps it is not so crazy as it seems. It is certainly not self-contradictory, as is so often said. A filmmaker can insert himself into his own film, can he not? He would then have a double role – coming in from outside and yet interacting with the other characters in the film.

Why cannot God do what Alfred Hitchcock did so often? God must be able to do anything that is intrinsically possible, and to come among us as one of us is both possible and meaningful if he wants to show us what he is like in the terms we best understand, the terms of a human life. In any case, who are we to tell such a God what he is not allowed to do? The question is not 'Is it possible?' but 'Is it true?'

There are probably only two people in all history who so astonished their contemporaries that the question they evoked was not 'Who is he?' but 'What is he?' They were Jesus and Buddha. The answers these two gave were exactly opposite. Buddha said unequivocally that he was a mere man, not divine. Jesus on the other hand did lay claim to sharing the nature of God. Of course he did not go round saying, 'I am divine,' but his actions and his claims pointed inexorably to that conclusion.

One of the ways he referred to himself was as 'Son' of God – that is, someone who is of the same nature as God. He called God his 'Father'. He said, 'I and the Father are one' (John 10.30) and, 'Whoever has seen me has seen the Father' (John 14.9). He claimed to reveal God accurately and enable anyone, through him, to know what God is like: 'No one knows the Son except the Father, and no one knows the Father except the Son, and anyone to whom the Son chooses to reveal him' (Matthew 11.27).

He claimed to be without sin – 'Which of you can convict me of sin?' – and got no reply (John 8.46). He claimed the divine right to forgive men their sins (Mark 2.5), and the Jewish leaders who were present cottoned on to the implications very fast; 'Who can forgive sins but God alone?' they asked themselves in fury.

He claimed the right to accept worship, which is properly due to God alone. When Thomas falls at his feet after the resurrection, convinced by the marks of his crucifixion, and exclaims, 'My Lord and my God,' Jesus does not rebuke him but calmly accepts it as his right (John 20.28). This is in striking contrast to the way both Peter and Paul recoiled in horror when people tried to worship them (Acts 10.25; 14.12-15).

The most decisive function which belongs to God is judgment. Yet here again Jesus seems to have claimed this as his right. 'The Father has committed all judgment to the Son,' he says (John 5.22). And in the famous parable of the sheep and the goats (Matthew 25.31ff.), it is Jesus who sits in judgment on the world at the climax of history. It is hard to escape the conclusion that Jesus himself claimed to share God's nature and functions.

In the Old Testament there are many promises that the God who rescued the Jews from Egypt would intervene again and bring about his kingdom among human beings. But there is another great strand in the Old Testament predicting that a descendant of the great king David would become the rescuer of the people. Jesus was the first to join these two strands together. Jesus, one of David's descendants, was bringing God's rescue and establishing God's kingly rule. His mission was God's intervention – no less.

The rest of the New Testament is emphatic on the subject. Mark's Gospel begins: 'The beginning of the gospel of Jesus Christ, the Son of God' (Mark 1.1). Matthew, at the start of his Gospel, is at pains to point out the significance of the name Jesus, which means 'God rescues' and the fact that his coming means

'Emmanuel', 'God is with us' (Matthew 1.18, 23). Luke introduces Jesus with the words, 'He will be great, and will be called the Son of the Most High' (Luke 1.32). John is more insistent still: 'No one has ever seen God. It is God the only Son who has made him known' (John 1.18). Claims like this resound through the New Testament. St Paul, that most passionate monotheist Jew, can nevertheless say of Jesus, 'In him the whole fullness of deity dwells bodily' (Colossians 2.9). The other New Testament writers all say much the same.

What convinced them that this penniless peasant-teacher shared the very nature of God? They certainly did not come to that conclusion easily. Remember that they were Jews, and over the centuries Jews had become so certain that there was only one God that they would cheerfully die for their belief, which in fact often happened under the Roman occupation. What made them believe that God had become incarnate and was their contemporary?

First, it was **the authority and content of his teaching** that made the impact. 'Love your enemies. Do good to those who despitefully use you' – this was revolutionary stuff. And he did not only teach it. He did it. As the soldiers were nailing him to the cross he cried, 'Father, forgive them, for they do not know what they are doing.' Jesus had the highest possible regard for the scriptures of the Old Testament, yet he was clear that his own teaching, which he attributed to his heavenly Father, surpassed it. 'Heaven and earth shall pass away but my words shall not pass away.' Needless to say, they haven't! No ethical advance has emerged in the two thousand years since his day which cannot be derived from his teaching. No higher conception of God, no more profound understanding of man. Nor has any error been found in his teaching. It is peerless stuff, quite literally incomparable.

Then there was **the quality of his life**. It is one thing to preach the highest standards but it is quite another to live that way yourself, yet all the evidence suggests that Jesus did precisely that. There is no hint anywhere in the surviving material about Jesus to suggest that he ever fell below his own highest standards. His love for all, his unselfishness, courage, perceptiveness, patience and generosity are plain for all to see in the pages of the Gospels. He had all the virtues known to humankind, and none of the vices: his life was a moral miracle, and people recognised it. As one New Testament writer put it, he was 'holy, blameless, unstained, separate from sinners.' Three times at his trial Pilate declared him innocent, as did the centurion in charge of the execution. So did those who knew him best. 'If we say that we have no sin,' wrote his disciple John, 'we deceive ourselves … But in him was no sin.'

A third feature which convinced them was **the claims he made**. We have glanced at three of them already – to forgive sins, to accept worship and to judge the world. There were many more. 'I am the resurrection and the life,' he said; 'I am the light of the world', 'I am the way and the truth and the life. Nobody comes to the Father except through me.' C.S. Lewis crisply expresses the point which must have been dawning on the disciples. In *Miracles* (p.32) he writes, 'The discrepancy between the depth and sanity of his moral teaching and the rampant megalomania which must lie behind his theological teaching unless he is indeed God has never been satisfactorily got over.'

Then there were **his miracles**. His enemies could not deny them and the Gospels are shot through with the conviction that the mighty acts of Jesus disclosed the personal agency of God. The records claim emphatically that Jesus healed the sick, cleansed lepers, exorcised demonic forces that were ruining human lives, fed a multitude from a few loaves, walked on water, and once or twice restored a further span of life to people who had recently died. All this would be literally incredible if he was just a man, but not at all incredible if he shared the nature of God. These were no conjuring tricks, no self-advertisement. They were the long-awaited indications that God's great day of rescue had dawned, that the majesty and glory of the living God were present (Isaiah

35.2-6; 61.1-4). His healing of a paralytic led the bystanders to say, 'We never saw anything like this' (Mark 2.12). His walking on water and stilling a storm had the same effect on his disciples in the boat. 'Who is this, that even the wind and sea obey him?' (Mark 4.41).

A further factor was **his fulfilment of centuries-old predictions** in the Jewish Bible. The Old Testament, so the Jews believed, enshrined the oracles of God. Yet it was manifestly incomplete. It spoke of a future king of David's stock whose dominion would be boundless. It spoke of one like a Son of Man coming from God and receiving a kingdom that would never be destroyed, together with power, great glory and universal sovereignty. It spoke of a prophet like Moses whose teaching would be unparalleled. It spoke of a Servant of the Lord whose death would atone for the sins of the people. It spoke of a new covenant between God and humanity which would place God's Spirit in human hearts so that they could know God personally and experience his power. It spoke of a coming prophet, priest and king who would be born in Bethlehem, to the royal line but of a humble family. He would both restore the faith of Israel and be a light to non-Jews. He would be put to death among evildoers but his tomb would be supplied by a rich man. He would live again, and the Lord's programme would prosper in his hand.

All of this came true with Jesus. Not some of it: all of it. There is no example in the history of the world where prophecies uttered centuries earlier in a holy book were fulfilled to the letter by a historical person in this way. It amazed his followers, but it convinced them. What do you make of it?

What finally convinced them was **the way he died and the fact that he rose again from the grave**. We shall be considering these two crucial points later. But despite their understandable disbelief that anyone could return from the grave, these erstwhile followers of Jesus, once convinced, were so passionate about their discovery that they spread the message wherever they went and the largest religion in the world was born.

It is a staggering thing to believe that Jesus could have brought God onto the stage of human life. But consider the alternative. Did the Gospel writers lie? If so, for what reason? To gain martyrdom? That is hardly an attractive temptation! Why did thousands gladly suffer torture and death for this faith if they knew it was untrue? What lie ever transformed human lives as the gospel message has done throughout two millennia? And if it was not a deliberate lie but a myth mistaken for literal truth, then who were these naïve fools that dreamed it up? There is nothing a Jew would be less likely to believe – that the transcendent God he worshipped should become a creature, a man, executed as a crucified criminal. Hardly a myth that springs naturally to the Jewish mind! And if it was not the Jews but the Gentiles who started the myth, how was it that all the first disciples were Jews, and that 25 of the 27 books in the New Testament were written by Jews?

Whoever it was that started the 'myth', they could not have done so in the lifetime of those who had known Jesus, for it would be publicly refuted by eyewitnesses.

But that is not what happened. The so-called 'myth' of Jesus' divinity goes back to those very contemporaries of his. The great Thomas Aquinas argued shrewdly that if Jesus did not embody God, then an even more incredible miracle happened – the conversion of vast swathes of the world by the biggest lie in history, and the moral transformation of countless lives to new heights of unselfishness, love and holiness by a mere myth. Not likely, is it?

Consider the facts for a moment. Can you seriously believe Jesus was a liar? He was unselfish, caring, passionate about the truth and leading others to the truth. Could such a man be a liar? And what possible motive could he have had? In any case he could not have hoped his 'lie' would be successful – Jews were the last people in the world to worship a man! The same cogent arguments would apply if it was not Jesus but his first followers who put out the 'lie'.

Is there any more mileage in supposing he was self-deceived, crazy? There have been crazy people in history thinking they were God. Could Jesus have been one of them? No, for a number of reasons. For one thing, lunatics lack the very qualities that shine out from Jesus – wisdom, creativity, tough love, profundity of insight. For another, a lunatic does not make you feel challenged, but rather embarrassed, whereas the inherent challenge of

Jesus is everywhere apparent in the Gospel stories. And the last thing a Jewish lunatic would do is to think he was God. Nowhere in the world was the distinction between the divine and the human so clearly drawn as in Judaism. In any case, even if the idea that he was a lunatic might help us with his remarkable claims, we cannot escape the quality of his life, his fulfilment of prophecy and his mighty works.

The fundamental problem for unbelief has always been the historical data. If Jesus is not divine, as Christians claim he is, then who is he, and how do we account for the contemporary evidence about him? A satisfactory reply has never been given.

five
sceptical about forgiveness
through the cross?

sceptical about forgiveness through the cross?

It was a bright spring day, a public holiday. The crowds were spilling out of the city to watch an entertainment – three men stripped naked and tortured to death by the most painful form of execution ever invented. And this particular occasion turned out to be the most famous execution in history: the crucifixion of Jesus of Nazareth.

A procession forces its way through the crowd, hitting people out of the way with the flat of their swords, for they are a detachment of Roman soldiers. Men stare.

Women weep. Children scuttle out of the way. Suddenly the central figure of the three comes into view. He is utterly exhausted after two trials, a sleepless night with his back lacerated from the cat-o-nine tails, and blood running into his eyes from the crown of thorns with two-inch spikes rammed onto his head. He staggers under the weight of the cross beam he is condemned to carry on his shoulders. He collapses, and cannot get up.

The officer in charge arrests an African bystander. 'You'll do. You carry his cross beam for him. Get moving.' They drag Jesus to his feet and the pitiful procession moves on to the nearby place of execution. The soldiers clear the crowd, fix the cross beams onto the uprights and nail the men to them through wrists and ankles. They jerk the crosses into pits already dug for them, and haul them upright with ropes.

The two criminals executed with Jesus struggled, cursed and doubtless urinated over their tormentors. But Jesus did not struggle. As we have seen, he prayed instead – 'Father, forgive them, they do not know what they are doing.' And sitting down they watched him there. The heat. The flies. The insults. The unspeakable agony in every nerve. The raging thirst. Crucifixion was a slow death. And as he hung there it grew dark, an uncanny darkness recorded by Thallus, a secular historian, writing a mere twenty years later. And out of the darkness, which reflected the darkness in the soul of Jesus, came a terrible cry of dereliction, 'My God, why?'

Why indeed? In a sense, I suppose, Jesus had it coming to him. Throughout the Gospel accounts we can see the opposition hardening from the religious authorities. They were jealous of his influence. They were fearful he would upset the tense political situation with the Roman overlords. They were livid that in showing God's love and healing people he broke their narrow religious prejudices. They were appalled that he seemed to set himself above the revered Law of Moses and even above the Temple. They were apoplectic that he claimed God as his Father. Yes, this man must perish. He had it coming to him.

But another strand runs through the story. Jesus had been uncompromising in unmasking the dark side of human nature as well as commending the good. He said, 'From within, out of men's hearts come evil thoughts, sexual immorality, theft, murder, adultery, greed, malice, deceit, envy, lewdness, slander, arrogance and folly. All these evils come from inside, and they defile a man' (Matthew 15.19-20). Blunt talk – but undeniable. The seeds of noxious weeds like these grow in the soil of every life, even if, mercifully, they have not all flowered. They defile us. They cut us off from God's presence. That is why God seems so far away, so unreal. Our words, our deeds, our thoughts and attitudes insulate us from God as effectively as heavy nimbus clouds separate us from the sun. And Jesus maintained throughout his ministry that he had come to rescue the alienated, to seek and save those who had lost their way. It would involve his death. That is why he went to Jerusalem knowing full well he would be betrayed, handed over to the chief priests and killed. He had an appointment with death. He said he had come to 'give his life as a ransom for many' (Mark 10.45). What a vivid analogy! It speaks as powerfully to the hijacking of our own day as it did to robbers who held men hostage in his. He saw humankind as captured, hijacked and held to ransom by the dark side of our nature, the evil within us. Our situation was desperate: enslaved by addictions and mired in guilt, we would perish unless a ransom was paid to set us free. Jesus saw his life, laid down in death, as that ransom, and that is why he so willingly trod the agonising path to Calvary.

What accounts for the fascination that central figure on his cross has exercised over two thousand years? Why is there a cross in every church and around many a neck? The answer does not lie simply in the physical torment, unspeakable though that was – the two brigands executed with him that very day met just as terrible an end. It does not even lie in the anguish of his mental suffering – with his life's work in ruins, deserted by his followers, betrayed by a friend, and rejected by the very people he had come to rescue. No, it was the spiritual sufferings of Jesus that take us to the heart of what his death entailed. Jesus, the perfect man, the sinless Son of God, allowed himself to be drowned in the foul tide of human wickedness so as to provide us with a lifeboat, saving us from the consequences of our folly, guilt and shame that are such an offence to God. It is as though all the wickedness of humanity throughout the ages was piled into a stinking dustbin and emptied over his willing head. My sins and yours included. He was determined to clear them out of the way by taking them on himself. That's why he went to the cross. That's why he felt cut off from his heavenly Father. He was cut off – for us. The dark clouds of human wickedness cut him off from the sunshine of the Father's love in which he had always basked. And he gladly endured it for us.

On the edge of the crowd that day skulked Simon Peter, the disciple who left Jesus in the lurch and swore he did not even know him. This is how Peter later explained what Jesus did on that cross: 'Christ has once and for all suffered for sins, the just for the unjust, to bring us to God' (1 Peter 3.18). That claim, although gloriously redemptive, prompts some questions, does it not? We are right to be sceptical on a number of points. Here are four that I commonly encounter.

Can guilt be transferred? A good question. I do not see how it can. But though guilt cannot be transferred, the consequences can … if someone loves you enough to face them in your place. On that terrible cross Jesus absorbed the consequences of human guilt. He took responsibility for the alienation, the separation from God, that you and I had incurred because of our misdeeds. Is that not simply matchless generosity?

Was atonement necessary? Surely God can just forgive? Why should any sacrifice be required? To be sure, a father can forgive his son … but a judge cannot forgive a criminal. If the man is guilty, the penalty must stand. God is both loving Father and incorruptible Judge. He is the moral ruler of the universe and he must show up evil for the monstrous thing it is. Like a judge he must disown it in the clearest possible terms. Yet because, as a Father, he loves us, he determined to take upon himself the consequences of the concentrated wickedness of the whole race. You can be sure that atonement was necessary for, if it was not, Jesus certainly would never have determined to go to the cross, that terrible place of judgment.

Was it fair? After all, the wrong person died – and Jesus had done no wrong. We can only answer this question once we understand, as the New Testament makes abundantly clear, that Jesus was both human and divine. United with humankind, he took the rap for all men and women. United with God, what he did there was more than fair. His self-sacrifice was sheer, undreamed-of generosity and it was effective for all who would avail themselves of it, both before and after the crucifixion itself. Sometimes people ask, 'What about the evil committed by those who lived before Jesus?' Those who trusted God's mercy then could be accepted because of what Jesus would do on the cross. We can be accepted because of what he has done there. With God there is no 'before' and 'after'.

Is forgiveness automatic? No. In the light of Calvary God offers forgiveness to all, but it is only effective when it is received with awe and gratitude. It takes two to tango!

There are three other characters who were present at Calvary on that spring day. Their experiences can tell us more about what the cross of Jesus means.

The freedom fighter

The first man was Barabbas, head of a terrorist group. He and his two colleagues had committed murder in the uprising, had been captured by the Romans and condemned to death. Imagine Barabbas in his cell, sweating with fear on that last morning of his life. Steps ring out down the corridor. A key grates in the lock. A warder comes in, knocks off his chains, and shouts, 'Get the hell out of here, Barabbas. You've been freed. Someone else is going to die on your cross. Scram!' Barabbas staggers out into the sunlight. In a daze, he walks out to the place of execution. Of course he does. He can't desert his friends. He looks at that central cross and mutters, 'That was my cross. I should have been there. This Jesus fellow is dying for me. He was innocent but he dies. I was guilty but I go free.' Incredible exchange! Matthew, Mark and Luke all tell us about Barabbas. They want us to understand this mind-boggling exchange, that Jesus took the place of the guilty so that the guilty could go free.

The executioner

As officer in charge of the execution, the centurion had the closest view of anyone on that grim occasion. He was deeply impressed by this dignified sufferer who prayed for his killers, did not think of himself but showed concern for others – his mother standing by and the criminals executed with him. The centurion had heard the mockery of the priests and had felt the uncanny darkness. He heard the great cry as Jesus died, 'Father into your hands I commend my spirit.' And he burst out with an amazing confession of faith in this person he had just executed. 'Truly this man was the Son of God.' What he meant by it is debatable, but as it was a title the emperor himself claimed, it reveals the centurion's profound reverence when he applies it to a crucified member of a subject race, which amounted to treachery to Rome. But we can hardly doubt how the Gospel writers saw it. 'Jesus Christ, Son of God, Saviour,' was the earliest creed at Christian baptism. Here was the very man who crucified Jesus making what became the Christian confession of faith!

I think we can be pretty sure about this. In the verses immediately before, the Gospel writers do a strange thing. They record Jesus' death, and then seem to ruin the climax by immediately introducing apparently irrelevant information: 'The curtain of the temple was ripped in half from top to bottom' (Mark 15.38), and then, after this detour, return us straight to Calvary and the centurion's confession of faith. What were they trying to convey?

The curtain in question was 60 feet high, designed to keep people out of the most holy part of the Temple, which was God's space alone. Nobody could enter it except the high priest once a year on the Day of Atonement after offering elaborate sacrifices for his own sins and those of the people of Israel. That curtain was a powerful visual aid. It meant 'Keep out. God is holy and you are not. No entry.' When Jesus died on the cross that curtain was ripped apart. Not as we would do it, from the bottom to the top. God split it from the top to the bottom. That clearly meant 'Come in'. The way into God's holy presence was now open, for Jesus had made the real sacrifice for the sins of the whole world which the Jewish sacrificial system had foreshadowed. That is what the Gospel writers want us to understand. The death of Jesus spells access to God for anyone who will take it.

The crucified murderer

The person hanging next to Jesus was an evil man. He had committed pillage and murder, and by the cruel standards of the day deserved his fate. He was facing imminent death and had only hours left. But in this extreme situation he was aware of God, and of the difference between right and wrong, as he rebukes his fellow criminal for his cynicism. Then, turning his head to Jesus, he says, 'Jesus, remember me when you come into your kingdom' (Luke 23.42). What astonishing faith! He believes that Jesus, dying next to him, has a future and might remember him. He believes Jesus has a kingdom! To turn to a bloodied, suffering man in his death throes and ask to be favourably remembered in the life to come is simply staggering. And Jesus replied with one of the greatest of his sayings. 'Truly I tell you, today you will be with me in paradise.' It would have been marvellous for that robber even to know he would die that day – often wretches lingered on their cross for a couple of days. More marvellous still, that he would be with Jesus. Marvellous to have that future described in a lovely old Persian word for a park, 'paradise', the happy part of the next world. But most marvellous of all is the implication which comes through loud and clear. This man's accusing past has been put away. His sins are forgiven, his guilt gone and his penalty dealt with. His future lies with Jesus in God's garden.

Three things are worth noticing. First, he had no good deeds to offer – he was an evil man. Second, he had no religious observances to offer – he died un-baptised, un-churched, but saved! Third, he had no time to amend his life. But he turned to Jesus with a prayer on his lips, confident that he could rely on Jesus for complete, though unmerited, pardon. The hymn puts it well: 'Nothing in my hand I bring, simply to your cross I cling.'

That is what the Gospel writers want us to understand from these graphic pen pictures of three men at the very heart of the action that Friday. Barabbas saw that Jesus went to the cross instead of him. The centurion saw that because Jesus died he could get through to God. And the murderer ended his life confident that his accusing past was swept away and that he would be with Jesus in God's garden. Substitution, access and pardon – that is what the cross of Jesus means for all who will avail themselves of it. And that, surely, calls for scepticism to give way to adoring gratitude.

six
sceptical about
the resurrection?

sceptical
about the
resurrection?

There is perhaps no area of Christian belief which is treated with such scorn by sceptics as the claim that Jesus was raised from the dead. Only yesterday I received a letter which included the following. 'Do me a favour. The next time he visits your centre as a full-bodied resurrected Jesus, not a meme virus embedded in the brain of an intellectually contaminated being, invite me round and I will call in and have tea with you. Of one thing we can be clinically sure. No living thing on becoming dead ever lives again.'

Let's pass over the 'meme' comment. It was one of Professor Dawkins' unwarranted ideas that nobody wants to talk about any more. But many share my correspondent's scepticism about the resurrection. I certainly used to.

I was a cheerful teenager, content with my home, my academic success and my sporting achievements, when I stumbled across the challenge of Jesus Christ. I was not an emotional cripple looking for a crutch. I was not a romantic looking for a cause. I was not looking for anything in particular. But I found treasure, and it has captivated my life. It happened like this.

One day when I was nearly 16, I was invited by a school friend to a somewhat subterranean Christian meeting in the school cricket pavilion. There were about 30 boys there. An elderly man was speaking. I recall his words to this day. 'Jesus Christ is alive, risen from the dead. You can know him.' In amazement I turned to the boy next to me, 'Who is that geezer?' He replied, 'Don't you know? He is Professor Rendle Short, professor of surgery here in the University of Bristol, and editor of the *British Medical Journal*.' I was utterly blown away. If he thought Jesus was alive from the grave he must be crazy. But if he edited the *BMJ* he could not be crazy. That was a massive dilemma. I was utterly sceptical, but I realised that if the resurrection was true it was the most momentous discovery I could ever make. If it was not true, Christianity was a fraud and I would pour my energies into unmasking it. So I determined to find out.

Before long I was examining the oldest written evidence on the subject, chapter 15 of the apostle Paul's first letter to Corinth. It runs like this:

> " I handed on to you as of first importance what I in turn had also received: that Christ died for our sins according to the scriptures, that he was buried, that he was raised on the third day in accordance with the scriptures, and that he appeared to Cephas, then to the twelve, then to more than 500 brothers at one time, most of whom are still alive, though some have died. Then he appeared to James, then to all the apostles. Last of all, as to someone untimely born, he appeared to me. For I am the least of the apostles, unfit to be called an apostle, because I persecuted the church of God. But by the grace of God I am what I am, and his grace towards me has not been in vain. … If Christ has not been raised, your faith is futile and you are still in your sins. Then those who have died in Christ have perished. If for this life only we have hoped in Christ, we are of all people most to be pitied. But in fact Christ has been raised from the dead, the first fruits of those who have died. " (1 Corinthians 15.3-20)

I encourage you to put aside apathy – if this stuff is true this is the most important topic you will ever handle. Put aside the idea that Christ's resurrection was borrowed from the ancient mystery religions – there is no single example in them of any person rising from the dead. And put aside the assumption that resurrection is scientifically impossible – that would not follow if Jesus really does share divine as well as human nature. In any case dogmatism is not the best way of solving a problem. Examining the evidence is.

Weigh the evidence

First, consider the man who wrote this. A massive intellectual, passionately anti-Christian, he killed believers wherever he could find them. But his life was completely turned round by the very thing he denied: the resurrection of Jesus from the grave. That encounter with Jesus on the Damascus Road transformed his life. 'Have I not seen the Lord?' he asked. No single fact, apart from Jesus himself, has been so significant for the spread of Christianity as the conversion of Saul the persecutor into Paul the apostle. That fact alone should make us sit up!

Next, consider the prominence he gives it. It is 'of first importance'. It is the very heart of Christianity, not some incidental feature of the Christian landscape. After all, what other religious leader has ever emerged from the tomb?

Next, note the date of the letter. It was written in AD 52, before any of the Gospels, and a mere twenty years after the event itself, not centuries later when myths could have grown. Hardly any ancient happening is supported by such good and early evidence. But we can go even further back.

Reflect on the age of the tradition. The words used for 'I received' and 'I passed on to you' are regularly used both in Greek and Hebrew for the transmission of authorised tradition. Paul received it from the first apostles and passed it on to the Corinthians when he preached the gospel to them in AD 50. Paul is claiming that this resurrection material had become authorised tradition in the Christian community by the time he received it at his conversion, which could not have been later than AD 35, that is to say within three years of the event itself. This is evidence of incalculable significance. No wonder the secular historian, Theodore Momsen, called the resurrection 'the best attested fact in ancient history'.

Consider the source of the tradition. Paul claims that his message of the resurrection is identical with that of the earliest disciples. He gives two names, James and Cephas. Cephas is the original Aramaic name for Peter, who claims that he was a witness of both cross and resurrection (1 Peter 5.1). He was one of the first to meet the risen Christ and be re-commissioned after his threefold denial of his master. After his extensive ministry and leadership of the new movement he was martyred for his faith. As for James, the resurrection had changed him from the sceptic that he was during Jesus' lifetime (John 7.5) into becoming the leader of the Jerusalem church – and subsequent martyrdom. You could not get two more reliable eyewitnesses than these.

The note of conviction is interesting. When Paul recounts that Jesus 'died', 'was buried' and 'appeared' he uses the Greek aorist, the tense to describe a simple past action. When he says 'he was raised' he interrupts the sequence of tenses and uses the perfect. And the perfect in Greek signifies an action in the past whose effects remain in the present. It means 'He rose and is alive'. What a fascinating sidelight on Paul's confidence in the risen presence of Jesus!

Assess the strength of the evidence. It is carefully tabulated.

1. 'Christ died.' Jesus was undoubtedly dead. You did not survive a Roman execution. An eyewitness testified to the 'blood and water' that emerged from Jesus' side when it was pierced by a soldier's spear to ensure he was dead (John 19.34). The witness could not possibly have known the medical fact that the separation of clot and serum is the strongest evidence of death. In any case, the confidence of the centurion in charge of the execution, and of Pilate the governor, both of whom had much to lose if wrong, is decisive.

Jesus was dead all right, and any theory which supposes that he was not, but revived in the cool of the tomb and escaped to an unrecorded future and nameless grave cannot stand critical scrutiny. Paul wants to remind his readers that, in fulfilment of the role of the Suffering

Servant of the Lord in Isaiah 53, Jesus died for our sins.

2. 'He was buried.' This is an allusion to the empty tomb. Nobody in the next 150 years denied that the tomb was found empty on the first Easter Day. The Jews would dearly have loved to rubbish the idea once the early Christian preaching of the resurrection began. How convenient it would have been to go to the tomb and show Jesus' body decomposing there. But nobody could.

The friends of Jesus could not have removed it – there was, after all, a guard on the tomb (Matthew 27.62-66) and the bedraggled disciples with shattered hopes were in no mood for elaborate hoaxes. They had scattered in terror when he was arrested and crucified. In any case, the idea that they stole the body, even had it been possible, is psychologically incredible. They were prepared to die for their belief in his resurrection, and many of them did. You do not die for something you know to be a hoax.

The soldiers could not have removed the body. They were there to ensure that it remained in place. They might face execution if they had failed in their duty.

As we have seen, the Jewish authorities would not have moved the body. They had been scheming for some time to get him dead and buried, and now they had succeeded.

The fact is that no naturalistic explanations of the resurrection have ever won much support, for the simple reason that none of them hold water. A charming touch which convinced Peter and John, when they ran to the sepulchre to see for themselves, was this. The shroud which had covered the body of Jesus and the separate head-covering remained in place while the body had disappeared (John 20.6-9). No human agent would dream of doing such a macabre thing. But if the body of Jesus was raised and transformed, rather as a solid, like coal, is transformed into energy, that explains why the graveclothes should have remained intact. The body was not there but the graveclothes were, like an abandoned chrysalis case when the butterfly has hatched.

3. 'Christ was raised.' That was the last thing any Jew could imagine. The Sadducees, an aristocratic party in Judaism, did not believe in any resurrection. The Pharisee party did, but only at the Last Day. The idea of a resurrection in the midst of history would have been inconceivable to anybody.

4. 'He appeared' to a whole stream of witnesses. This of course is how you establish any historical event. You cannot prove something like the date of the Battle of Hastings by logic alone, but you can amass so much eyewitness testimony that only the prejudiced would refuse to credit it.

The empty tomb alone would never have given rise to the Easter faith. It would have been just a puzzle. But something happened which explained why the tomb was empty and sent his friends onto the streets delirious with joy. That something was the repeated appearances of Jesus, alive again, for a limited period of six weeks, to convince his followers that the unthinkable had

happened, and that the last Enemy had been overcome. He appeared first to Cephas (i.e. Peter), then to the twelve disciples, then to a crowd of '500 at one time', presumably in Galilee where most of his ministry had taken place. Then he appeared to 'all the apostles' – including Thomas who had been absent when Jesus first showed himself to his disciples a week earlier. Thomas, the rather admirable hard-headed sceptic, had refused to believe his colleagues when they claimed to have seen Jesus alive again. But now he falls at Jesus' feet in worship and acclaims him as, 'My Lord and my God' (John 20.26ff.).The last of those resurrection appearances, recorded here in 1 Corinthians 15, was to the writer, Paul himself.

Some have tried to explain these appearances as hallucinations, but it will not do. Hallucinations happen to particular personality types, and are usually associated with particular locations. They persist, and make for the disintegration of personality. These appearances happened to all types of personality in a variety of locations. They lasted only 40 days and they led, not to disintegration, but to profound joy and wholeness.

5. There is a further factor to bear in mind. The changed lives of the disciples stare us in the face, not only in this passage but throughout the New Testament. Peter was transformed from a coward into a man or rock and a martyr. The twelve were changed from a frightened rabble into a fearless church. Paul was changed from rabid persecutor to fearless apostle. James was changed from sceptic to Christian leader. Indeed, you could rightly say that the church began on Easter Day. It cannot be traced back any earlier than that.

The church was launched by the resurrection.

Of course the disciples were initially slow to believe it (who wouldn't be?) but, once convinced, their message spread like wildfire throughout the empire. Their only difference from Judaism was Jesus himself, Jesus crucified and risen!

Yes, the evidence is compelling. It fully persuaded me in my teenage search, and over many years as a New Testament scholar I have studied it intensively. No wonder Sir Edward Clarke, a High Court Judge, said, 'As a lawyer I have made a prolonged study of the evidence for the events of Easter Day. The evidence is conclusive. Over and over in the High Court I have secured a verdict on evidence not nearly so compelling.'

Reflect on the implications

Just think what this means. It answers *three of the toughest intellectual questions* we could ever ask. Does God exist? Which religion? What happens after death?

The resurrection demonstrates the existence of God, validates the religion of Jesus, and shows there is a life after death. Jesus is indeed 'the firstfruits of those who died,' as 1 Corinthians 15 puts it.

The resurrection also has something very important to say to *three of the most pressing personal issues* we ever face.

What about my accusing past? The stuff I have done that I can't get out of my mind? The playwright Arthur Miller said, 'The birds come home to roost. You do something, and you try to undo it – but it won't undo. It keeps pursuing you until it catches up with you.' True, is it not? The cross and resurrection are the cure for that. The apostle Paul again: 'Christ was delivered up for our offences and raised because of our acquittal.' That makes such a difference. I recall a wartime sniper who told me of his terrible nightmares because he had shot many people. He came to see that his guilt before God had been cancelled by what Jesus did on the cross. He put his trust in Jesus – and the nightmares disappeared.

What about my present situation? The loneliness, the pressure, the fears? The risen Christ does not remove them, but promises his companionship in the midst of them. He says to his followers, 'I am with you always, even to the end of the world,' and countless believers have proved the truth of it. I know I have.

Then there is the future. Uncertainty about employment, retirement, death? Listen to the apostle Paul again. 'Who shall separate us from the love of Christ? Will hardship or distress or persecution, or famine or sword? ... No, in all these things we are more than conquerors through him who loved us. For I am convinced that neither death nor life, nor angels nor rulers, nor things present nor things to come, nor powers, nor height nor depth, nor anything else in all creation, will be able to separate us from the love of God in Christ Jesus our Lord.' (Romans 8.35-39). Even death loses much of its terror. Maria, a Russian nun, walked voluntarily into the Nazi gas chamber in Ravensbruck concentration camp, to accompany a terrified girl. 'Christ is risen,' she said, taking her arm. 'There is nothing to fear.'

So there you have it. The evidence that Jesus is risen from the dead is powerful. The relevance of that risen Jesus to our human lives is overwhelming and available for us all.

And this brings me back to that cricket pavilion in Bristol where I first heard that Jesus was alive, but was extremely sceptical about it. I made my investigation both into the historical evidence and into the demeanour of the boys who claimed to know this Jesus. And one day Richard Gorrie, the leader of that unofficial Christian meeting, challenged me. 'Now that you have looked into

it, do you believe that Jesus Christ rose from the dead?'
'I think I do,' I said. 'In which case, he is alive and you can meet him,' he replied. 'What are you going to do about him?' He then showed me a verse that transformed my life. I have seen it transform the lives of many other sceptics since then. It could do as much for you, too. He pointed to a remarkable promise of the risen Jesus. 'Behold, I stand at the door and knock. If any one hears my voice and opens the door I will come in' (Revelation 3.20). Jesus was willing to come and partner me in life. I saw that it was not just a question of my intellect but of my will.

That day I drew back the bolts which had kept the door of my life locked fast in scepticism and self-centredness. I prayed. I told Jesus Christ that I was ashamed at having kept him excluded for so long. I asked him to come into my life, by his unseen Spirit, to share it with me and start to make a difference. That was only the beginning, of course. But it was by far the most important decision I have ever made. It was the indispensable launch into a lifelong partnership. Sixty-five years later I can only look back with gratitude … and I can face old age and death with confidence.

seven
sceptics who changed
their minds

sceptics
who changed
their minds

It's no bad thing to be sceptical. It saves you taking on board a load of rubbish. But by the same token it is no bad thing to revoke your scepticism and change your mind, if the evidence you have been looking into warrants it.

I submit to you that the evidence outlined in this short book is sufficient to give honest sceptics grounds for changing their minds. There is more than enough to indicate that Jesus really did bring God onto the scene of human life, that he died for our sins, and that he is risen from the grave and available for us to encounter. In the light of this evidence, countless sceptics down the centuries have risked entrusting their lives to him despite some nagging areas of doubt.

Early sceptics who changed their minds

It started with Jesus' own family who were highly sceptical. As we have seen, they did not believe in him when he was engaged in his public ministry. Later, after the resurrection, that all changed. His brother James became the leader of the Jerusalem church, and he was succeeded by another brother, Jude. They had the courage to face up to the evidence and change their mind about Jesus, even though it must have involved massive loss of face. It would have caused much merriment in the pubs at Nazareth!

We have also seen that another highly intelligent contemporary, Saul of Tarsus, was a pronounced sceptic about Jesus to the extent that he hunted down members of this new sect to kill them. But he too changed his mind when he came face to face with the risen Jesus on that road to Damascus, and his conversion changed the history of the world.

Throughout the centuries the same thing keeps happening. Early in the second century we find a sceptical professional philosopher, Justin, coming to trust Christ through the combined testimony of an old Christian man that he met and 'the terrible power of the scriptures'. After his conversion he continued as a philosopher, keeping on his lecturer's gown as he maintained to all and sundry that Jesus was the summit of the philosophical quest. Augustine in the fourth century was a long-time sceptic, but came to a full-blooded Christian faith at the end of an extended search and turned into one of the most significant figures in human history.

Recent sceptics who changed their minds

C.S. Lewis

There are many in recent times who have trodden the same path. None is more famous than the convinced Oxford atheist, C.S. Lewis. Immensely able and intelligent, Lewis tells us in *Mere Christianity* that his main argument against God was that the universe seemed so cruel and unjust.

> But how had I got this idea of just and unjust? A man does not call a line crooked unless he has some idea of a straight line. What was I comparing the universe with when I called it unjust? Thus in the very act of trying to prove that God did not exist – in other words that the whole of reality was senseless – I found I was forced to assume that one part of reality, namely my idea of justice, was full of sense. Consequently atheism turns out to be too simple. If the whole

universe has no meaning, we should never have found out that it has no meaning. 🙶

Here was a truly honest sceptic who was prepared to doubt his doubts. It was a major step on the path to Christian discipleship. His own account of it in *Surprised by Joy* reads:

> In the Trinity term of 1929 I gave in and admitted that God was God, and knelt and prayed: perhaps, that night, the most dejected and reluctant convert in all England. I did not then see what is now the most shining and obvious thing; the Divine humility which will accept a convert even on such terms. The Prodigal Son at least walked home on his own feet. But who can duly adore that Love which will open the high gates to a prodigal who is brought in kicking, struggling, resentful, and darting his eyes in every direction for a chance of escape? 🙶

Lots of us sceptics felt like that when the Hound of Heaven caught up with us and we were constrained to change our minds! Lewis came to full trust in Jesus a couple of years later, in 1931, as he wrote to a friend:

> I have just passed on from believing in God to definitely believing in Christ – in Christianity. My long night talk with Dyson and Tolkien had a lot to do with it. 🙶

Many of us have been helped to discover Christ for ourselves through friends like that. And in another letter to a friend he wrote with great wisdom about his excitement when he gave in to Jesus Christ.

> It is quite right that you should feel that 'something terrific' has happened to you. Accept these sensations with thankfulness, as birthday cards from God, but remember that they are only greetings, not the real gift. The real thing is the gift of the Holy Spirit.
>
> Don't imagine that it is all 'going to be an exciting adventure' from now on. It won't. Excitement, of whatever sort, never lasts. This is the push to start you off on your bicycle: you'll be left to lots of dogged pedalling later on. And no need to feel depressed about it either. It will be good for your spiritual leg muscles.

That was shrewd advice.

Chuck Colson

Countless men and women have trod this path from scepticism to faith, men like Pascal, John Newton, G.K. Chesterton, Malcolm Muggeridge, Aleksandr Solzhenitsyn.

One of the celebrated sceptics I had the privilege of getting to know was Charles 'Chuck' Colson. From 1969 to 1973 he was Special Counsel to President Nixon. He was a hard, sceptical, arrogant man, described as Nixon's 'evil genius'. He occupied the office next to the President in the White House and swore he would be willing to walk over his grandmother to get Nixon re-elected. Then one night he had dinner with Tom Phillips, a friend who challenged him about his lifestyle and his scepticism, and gave him a slim book to read, written, as it happens, by none other than C.S. Lewis. It was *Mere*

Christianity. He sat and read it under a street light that night, embarrassed that his wife might see him with such a book if he read it at home. It made sense, and it led him to Christ.

Shortly afterwards he was arraigned for his part in the Watergate affair, pleaded guilty and went to prison for seven months, where his Christian faith blossomed. 'Bless you, prison, for having been in my life,' he would often exclaim. When he came out, he ended a life of accomplishment as a politician and began a life of significance as the most effective social reformer in the twentieth century. Not only did he become a skilled Christian apologist but he founded the Prison Fellowship, which is the largest compassionate outreach to prisoners in the world, and now ministers in over one hundred countries. Real 'conversion' or 'turning around' transforms a person's life and ambitions. Certainly Chuck Colson became a far more influential figure through his ministry to prisoners than he ever had been when a ruthless and sceptical politician.

Terrorists – and students

Tom Tarrants is another very interesting acquaintance of mine. He was a sceptic, an anti-Semite and a terrorist. Full of violence and hatred, he was profoundly opposed to desegregation in the American South in the 1960s, and by the age of 21 was a fully fledged member of the White Knights, the most dangerous wing of the Ku Klux Klan. He took part in some thirty bombings of churches, synagogues and homes. He was captured in a shootout with the FBI and police in which his partner was killed and he himself almost died after being shot 19 times. He was sentenced to thirty years in one of the roughest prisons in the US. With limited reading matter available he began to examine the Gospels. He was haunted by the words of Jesus. 'What shall it profit a man if he gains the whole world and loses his own soul?' Alone in his cell, he entrusted his broken life to Jesus Christ, and the transformation was very soon apparent. He renounced his membership of the Klan, and his deep-seated characteristic of hatred became changed into one of love. He is now one of the most gracious and gentle men I know. After release from prison he trained for Christian ministry, was ordained and has devoted himself to Christian work in the Washington DC area where he has been a university chaplain, a director of the School for Urban Mission and for some years President of the C.S. Lewis Institute. He has a particular gift in sensitive counselling. Tom is an outstanding example of the difference Jesus Christ makes to life when a person turns from scepticism to surrender.

Moving from US law courts to the British university scene, the flow of sceptics becoming committed Christians continues. **Pete Nicholas** went up to Oxford to read Philosophy, Politics and Economics in 1997. He was very sceptical about Christianity. He did not believe it would stand up intellectually, or provide a consistent framework for human knowledge. In any case it would be restrictive! A passionate sportsman, he trained for three years preparing for a big rugby match (Oxford versus Cambridge), in which he played … and won. And yet he found a pervading sense of emptiness. 'It really confused me,' he wrote to me. 'Why wasn't I happier?' He continued the story:

> At the same time I had attended a week of talks during the university mission and started to see, not only that Christianity did have answers to life's big questions, but – more surprisingly, that the answers were often uniquely compelling. Quickly what had been of passing interest took centre stage, and so I took a few weeks out of revising for my finals to see who Jesus was and what it meant to follow him. The more I read the more I became convinced of his life, death and resurrection, not just in some abstract way but in a deeply personal way that I knew was for me. He had lived the life I should live, and he died the death I deserved to die. And so in April 2000 I committed myself to follow him.

Pete has been training for ordination as a vicar, and is

preparing to start a new church in London while continuing to work with Christians in Sport. He concludes, 'What a change – but what a privilege.'

Another friend, **Steve Collier**, who has recently finished postgraduate work and been ordained, writes as follows.

> During my teens I became increasingly sceptical, and aggressively rejected Christianity on three grounds. One, that it was, in the words of Karl Marx, 'the opiate of the people'. It acted as a sedative for those who could not handle the harsh realities of life. Two, that religion was the catalyst for so much that is wrong in the world. And three, that there is no evidence for the existence of a God.
>
> And now I am an ordained minister in the church. What has happened? When I was a student, aged 20, I surprised myself by accepting an invitation to go to a London Church -- Holy Trinity, Brompton. My expectations were not high. But that night changed my life. The preacher spoke of his Christian faith and the bad things he once saw in Christianity – which were very similar to my own objections. Then, all of a sudden, I realised the very simple truth that the Christian faith is about the person of Jesus. No more and no less. Immediately a veil was lifted from my eyes. All that time I had disliked and distrusted religion, I had been looking at the structures, the hierarchies, the

people who did not represent it well … and had missed the point. I hadn't recognised the person of Jesus for who he is. When I did, everything changed. What more could I ask for as evidence of God than the Son of God himself? Since I committed myself to Jesus, my life has been transformed from one of wandering in the wilderness to one of loving relationship and joyful service as an ordained minister. To know, love and be in fellowship with Jesus is what we were created for, and that alone brings the most heartfelt joy. 🙵🙵

An Oxford Professor

Professor Alister McGrath is one of today's most lucid and persuasive Christian speakers and writers. He is a prolific and celebrated author and has debated with atheists including Richard Dawkins and Christopher Hitchens, as well as being in demand as a lecturer all around the world. He has doctorates both in the Natural Sciences and in Theology, has had the rare distinction of a personal Chair in Oxford University, and is currently a Professor of Theology at King's College, London. It will be a surprise to many that he was once an atheist, highly sceptical of Christianity, and is one of many who have come to a robust and highly intelligent Christian faith. He is a personal friend, and gladly contributed to this chapter as follows:

During the late 1960s, a surge of secularist euphoria swept across Western Europe and North America. In April 1966, *Time* magazine's cover story was the death of God. Sociologists were predicting the dawn of a new secular era, in which belief in God would die out and be replaced by secular ideologies, such as Marxism. Religion would be swept aside as at best an irrelevance to real life, and at worst an evil, perverse force which enslaved humanity through its lies and delusions.

That was the cultural mood of the late 1960s. And I shared it. Marxism was the oxygen of the cultural atmosphere of the day throughout much of Western Europe at this time, even in my own native Northern Ireland. Yet for me, the Marxist critique of religion was supplemented by something just as powerful and persuasive – the scientific view of reality.

Science explained everything. It gobbled up the conceptual space once occupied by God, and replaced it with the sane, cool rationalism of the scientific method. Only scientific claims are meaningful. The sciences were, for me, the only true way to acquire reliable knowledge about reality and the order of things. Atheism was my creed, and science was its foundation.

I won a scholarship to Oxford University to study

chemistry, seeing this as both immensely satisfying in its own right, and also as a means of consolidating and extending my atheism. While preparing to go up to Oxford, however, I began to read works dealing with the history and philosophy of science. This did not work out as I expected. I was assaulted with ideas that battered at the roots of my atheist faith. I could no longer sustain the simplistic idea that 'science proves its ideas'. It was all much more complicated. I realised that you could believe things without being able to prove them. Then the penny dropped. Wasn't that what Christians were saying as well?

The seeds of doubt were planted in my mind. Was my atheism really some kind of logical fallacy based on a misunderstanding of the proper scope of science, or the nature of scientific claims? It was a deeply unsettling thought, and I tried not to think about it. Nobody likes their personal world of meaning to be disturbed too much. I was tempted to dismiss this sort of stuff in much the same way that Richard Dawkins still does – as ignorant, unscientific 'truth-heckling'. But my doubts would not go away.

When I arrived at Oxford in October 1971 I decided to look into these things properly, to set my mind at rest. I expected to find my atheism reinforced, so that I could dismiss such intellectual distractions. I wanted closure of this question, so that I could get on with more important things. Yet while I had been severely critical of Christianity, I realised that I had yet to extend that same critical evaluation to atheism, tending to assume that it was self-evidently correct, and was hence exempt from being assessed in this way. During October and November 1971, I began to discover that the intellectual case for atheism was rather less substantial than I had supposed. Far from being self-evidently true, it seemed to rest on rather shaky foundations. Christianity, on the other hand, turned out to be far more robust than I had supposed. It made sense! And it was exciting, both intellectually and spiritually!

Finally, I realised that atheism was actually a belief system, where I had assumed it to be a factual statement about reality. In the end, I turned my back on one faith, and embraced another. I turned away from one belief system that tried to deny it was anything of the sort, and accepted another which was quite open and honest about its status. My conversion was an act of free-thinking. I believed I had found the best way of making sense of things. And that remains my view today. I would now sum up my new faith in some words of C.S. Lewis: 'I believe in Christianity as I believe that the sun has risen – not just because I see it, but because by it I see everything else.'